Praise for the Believe Series

"As grandparents of fifty grandchildren, we heartily endorse the *Believe and You're There* series. Parents and grandparents, gather your children around you and discover the scriptures again as they come alive in the *Believe and You're There* series."

—STEPHEN AND SANDRA COVEY
Stephen Covey is the bestselling author of *7 Habits of Highly Effective People*

"Bravo! This series is a treasure! You pray that your children will fall in love with and get lost in the scriptures just as they are discovering the wonder of reading. This series does it. Two thumbs way, way up!"

—MACK AND REBECCA WILBERG
Mack Wilberg is the music director of the Mormon Tabernacle Choir

"This series is a powerful tool for helping children learn to liken the scriptures to themselves. Helping children experience the scriptural stories from their point of view is genius."

—ED AND PATRICIA PINEGAR
Ed Pinegar is the bestselling author of *Raising the Bar*

"We only wish these wonderful books had been available when we were raising our own children. How we look forward to sharing them with all our grandchildren!"

—STEPHEN AND JANET ROBINSON
Stephen Robinson is the bestselling author of *Believing Christ*

"The *Believe and You're There* series taps into the popular genre of fantasy and imagination in a wonderful way. Today's children will be drawn into the reality of events described in the scriptures. Ever true to the scriptural accounts, the authors have crafted delightful stories that will surely awaken children's vivid imaginations while teaching truths that will often sound familiar."

—TRUMAN AND ANN MADSEN
Truman Madsen is the bestselling author of *Joseph Smith, the Prophet*

"My dad and I read *At the Miracles of Jesus* together. First I'd read a chapter, and then he would. Now we're reading the next book. He says he feels the Spirit when we read. So do I."

—CASEY J., AGE 9

"My mom likes me to read before bed. I used to hate it, but the *Believe* books make reading fun and exciting. And they make you feel good inside, too."

—KADEN T., AGE 10

"Reading the *Believe* series with my tweens and my teens has been a big spiritual boost in our home—even for me! It always leaves me peaceful and more certain about what I believe."

—GLADYS A., AGE 43

"I love how Katie, Matthew, and Peter are connected to each other and to their grandma. These stories link children to their families, their ancestors, and on to the Savior. I heartily recommend them for any child, parent, or grandparent."

—ANNE S., AGE 50
Mother of ten, grandmother of nine (and counting)

When the Night Stayed Bright as Day

Books in the *Believe and You're There* series

VOLUME 1
When the White Dove Descended

VOLUME 2
At the Miracles of Jesus

VOLUME 3
When the Stone Was Rolled Away

VOLUME 4
When the Prince of Peace Was Born

VOLUME 5
When Lehi Left Jerusalem

VOLUME 6
When Ammon Was a Missionary

VOLUME 7
When the Night Stayed Bright as Day

Believe and You're There

When the Night
Stayed Bright as Day

Book 7

ALICE W· JOHNSON & ALLISON H· WARNER

DESERET
BOOK

Salt Lake City, Utah

Library of Congress Cataloging-in-Publication Data
Johnson, Alice W.
  Believe and you're there when the night stayed bright as day / Alice W. Johnson and Allison H. Warner ; illustrated by Jerry Harston and Casey Nelson.
    p. cm.
  Summary: Katie, Matthew, and Peter have further adventures by traveling through Grandma's paintings, this time in the lands of the Book of Mormon at the time of the sign of Jesus' birth.
  ISBN 978-1-60641-249-7 (paperbound)
  1. Jesus Christ—Nativity—Juvenile literature. 2.Book of Mormon stories. I. Warner, Allison H. II. Harston, Jerry. III. Nelson, Casey (Casey Shane), 1973– IV. Title.
  BT315.3.J625 2010
  232.92—dc22   2009038543

Printed in the United States of America
R. R. Donnelley and Sons, Crawfordsville, IN

10   9   8   7   6   5   4   3   2   1

Believe in the wonder,
Believe if you dare,
Believe in your heart,
Just believe . . . and you're there!

Contents

CHAPTER ONE

A New Painting 1

CHAPTER TWO

Zarahemla, Here We Come! 7

CHAPTER THREE

The Lamanite Prophet 15

CHAPTER FOUR

The Robbers' Raid 22

CHAPTER FIVE

Caleb's Conversion 32

CHAPTER SIX

A Murder Solved 39

CHAPTER SEVEN

The Return of Samuel 47

CHAPTER EIGHT

    A Narrow Escape 53

CHAPTER NINE

    In Five Years' Time 58

CHAPTER TEN

    When the Night Stayed Bright as Day 66

CHAPTER ELEVEN

    Home Again 76

Chapter One

A New Painting

"Mom! Mom!" hollered Katie as she hung up the phone and ran to find her mother. "Mom, where are you?"

"I'm down here in the basement," answered her mother as she started up the stairs with a basket of laundry. Reaching the top, she almost collided with Katie, who came flying around the banister with breathless energy.

"Mom! There you are!" Katie exclaimed. "Guess what? Grandma just called to say that she has finished another scripture painting! She wants the boys and me to come over after dinner to see the painting and hear the story that goes with it. Please, Mom. Please say yes!"

"You and Matthew and Peter have become very

interested in Grandma's paintings, haven't you?" Mother commented with curiosity.

"I guess we've just got good taste," laughed Katie, her deep dimple showing as she teased.

"Oh, is that it?" Mother teased right back. "I thought maybe Grandma just spoiled you rotten!" She put an affectionate arm around her thirteen-year-old daughter.

Katie hugged her in return, relieved that the questions seemed to have stopped. What would her mother think if she knew Grandma's scripture paintings whisked them away to the scene depicted? How would she feel about Katie and her younger brothers visiting faraway places in long ago times?

"Can we go, Mom?" pleaded Katie. "Can we go tonight?"

"Well, if you practice your flute and help me clean up the dishes quickly after dinner, I suppose I can take you over."

"Thanks, Mom. You're the best," Katie said, and she meant it.

Just then Matthew, age ten, appeared at the

back door, home from soccer practice. "Hey, Katie, what's up?"

"Great news, Matthew! Grandma just called to say that she's finished another painting!" Katie answered.

Matthew lit up. "When can we go? Have you asked Mom? Does Peter know? What is the painting of?"

"Slow down!" Katie laughed. "I can only answer one question at a time. Mom said we could go tonight if we clean up dinner in record time. And I don't know what story the painting's from."

"I'll be a cleaning tornado!" declared Matthew. "Does Peter know?"

"I haven't had a chance to tell him yet. He's in the backyard playing with his guinea pig," Katie replied.

"I'll go tell him. He's going to be so-o-o excited," called Matthew over his shoulder as he banged the screen door and headed out to find his eight-year-old brother.

Meanwhile, Katie dialed Grandma's number and waited for her to answer. One ring, two rings. Where was she? Three rings, four rings. Katie

fidgeted nervously. Five rings, six—and finally, Grandma's voice!

"Hello," she said.

"Grandma, it's Katie! We can come!"

"Wonderful! How does 6:30 sound?"

"It sounds great. That won't give us much time to do the dinner dishes, but we were planning to set a record anyway," said Katie.

"And I'll just bet you'll do it!" chuckled Grandma. "Come straight to the cottage, darling. I'll be waiting!" Click. And Katie skipped off to find her flute.

At 6:35, Mom finally turned the family car onto Grandma's street.

"Faster, Mom, faster!" Peter coaxed. "We're going to be late!"

"Late for what?" their mother questioned as she pulled into the driveway. "You're just visiting Grandma. What's the rush?"

"I guess we're just super-excited to see her," Peter was quick to explain, his eyes wide and innocent.

"If I didn't know better, I'd think you kids were

keeping something from me," Mother mused, bringing the car to a stop.

"Oh, Mom. Don't worry. We just love our grandma," the three children reassured their mother loudly as they scrambled out of the car. Then, as if it were a chore, each of the children kissed their mom and dutifully waved as she drove away.

Mother shook her head in puzzlement as she steered the car toward home. What could possibly be so exciting about an evening with Grandma?

Chapter Two

Zarahemla, Here We Come!

Mother would have been even more baffled if she had seen the children make a beeline for the backyard, giggling and teasing each other with eager anticipation. Across the lawn, behind the house, through the garden, along the flag-stone path . . . and there it was! Grandma's art cottage! Nestled in a grove of pine trees, the tiny white building beckoned with soft yellow light glowing from every window in the grey dusk of sunset.

The children rapped politely on the arched blue door and prepared to recite the special poem that would grant them entrance.

Grandma, dressed in a painter's smock covered with splotches of every hue, flung open the door to

7

the tiny house she used as her art studio. But she didn't step out. "Welcome, darlings," she said warmly, standing just inside the door. "I can't wait to hug you! But don't think for a moment that you'll get into this cottage without our password. Who's first?"

"I am," replied Matthew, and he took his place on the stoop, ready to recite the first line of the enchanted words Grandma had inscribed in the front of their special journals.

"Believe in the wonder," he intoned, a touch of mystery in his voice. He turned to Katie, who picked up the verse readily.

"Believe if you dare."

Peter needed no prompting. "Believe in your heart," he chanted.

And Grandma, as usual, joined all three children for the last line. "Just believe," four voices rang out, "and you're there!"

"Come in, dear children!" cried Grandma as she wrapped her arms around each grandchild in turn and ushered each through the door. Finally she loosened her last bear hug, and they were all inside.

The children looked around the studio. Right next to the fireplace stood Grandma's easel, covered with a draped white blanket.

Grandma busied herself with blankets and pillows on the floor in front of the covered easel. "Did you all remember your journals?" she asked.

"I have them all right in here," Katie said, pulling from her backpack the three special books Grandma had given them to record what they learned from their visits.

"We're all set then. Everyone get comfortable, and imagine that you're . . . here!" Grandma exclaimed as she lifted the blanket, unveiling a colorful, busy scene.

"Aa-a-ahh!" The children exhaled in unison.

"Wow!" breathed Peter. "Look at all the arrows flying. I've always wanted a bow and arrow, but Mom never lets me get one!"

"Can you blame her?" mumbled Katie, never taking her eyes from the easel.

"Hey!" said Matthew, as if he'd just made a great discovery. "This painting is of Samuel the Lamanite, isn't it, Grandma?"

"Well," said Grandma with admiration, "that sure didn't take you long, Matthew-boy! Bravo!"

"Samuel the prophet!" repeated Katie.

"He was a prophet?" questioned Peter. "But how could a Lamanite be a prophet?"

"I think I know just where we can find the answer to your question," Grandma declared. And

with that, she picked up her Book of Mormon and settled into her chair. Then she began to read:

"'And now it came to pass in the eighty and sixth year, the Nephites did still remain in wickedness . . . while the Lamanites did observe strictly to keep the commandments of God . . .'"

"Now wait just a minute," interrupted Peter. "That's not right—the Nephites were the righteous ones!"

"Not in this story," explained Katie. "This takes place about six hundred years after Lehi and his family left Jerusalem. A lot of things have changed since then, and now the Nephites are the really wicked ones. They have turned away from Heavenly Father, and the Lamanites are trying hard to obey the commandments."

"I didn't know that!" said Peter.

Matthew was becoming impatient with Peter's interruptions. "Peter," he said, "can't you just listen to the story? It will explain everything, you know."

"Okay, okay. Sorry," said Peter, looking a little glum.

Katie quietly put her arm around him, winked,

and whispered in his ear, "Sit right by me, buddy. Let's keep our eyes on the painting, shall we?"

"Oh, yeah!" said Peter, remembering what they were waiting for.

"I'll hurry," Grandma promised as she resumed reading. "'And it came to pass that in this year there was one Samuel, a Lamanite, came into the land of Zarahemla, and began to preach unto the people. . . .'"

Katie sat with her eyes glued to the painting, not daring even to blink in case she missed the slightest movement. She strained her neck forward, hoping with all her might that this painting would hold another adventure.

"'And it came to pass that he did preach, many days, repentance unto the people . . .'" Grandma continued.

"O-o-ohh!" Katie gasped. Her head moved closer to the painting.

Matthew heard Katie's sound of surprise and leaned in to get a closer look. What he saw made his heart stand still. There, above the wall around Zarahemla, a tiny arrow was sailing through the air.

And beneath it, people scattered to get out of its way!

Katie looked thoughtfully at Matthew. They both knew what this meant. Then she slowly mouthed the words, "Shall—we—go?"

In reply, Matthew nodded his head resolutely, his heart beating so loudly he was afraid Grandma would hear it. Katie reached for his hand, and with it firmly in her grasp, she used her other hand to grab Peter's.

Then Matthew, his finger quivering with antici-pation, reached out to the painting. And just like before, his finger disappeared into the canvas. As he pushed it further in, a giant schlooping sound engulfed the children, and they were sucked into the canvas, swallowed up by the scene before them.

Katie, Matthew, and Peter, their hands still en-twined, felt themselves carried away—away from the time they knew so well, away from Grandma's steady voice, away from the safe, warm cottage.

"Yahoo! We're flying again!" shouted Peter, his eyes full of daring and wonder.

"We sure are!" Katie sang out. "And I'll just bet

we're in for another great adventure!" Then she hollered joyfully, "Zarahemla, here we come!"

And yelling into the wind, the boys echoed their sister, "Zarahemla! Zarahemla! He-e-ere we-e-e come!"

Chapter Three

The Lamanite Prophet

After just a few thrilling moments of effortless flight, the ground came into view. The children clung to one another as they gently descended and then felt the ground beneath their feet. Looking around, they discovered they were near a tall stone wall that was so long it curved out of sight in the distance.

"This must be the wall that surrounds the city," said Matthew. "And look over there. It's an open gate leading in. Come on, let's go!"

"Wait just a minute," said Katie cautiously. "Do you really think we should go into a city where we've never been?"

"Uhh, why did we come, Sis, if we're not going to go in?" asked Matthew with a grin.

"Yeah," Peter chimed in. "I'm not staying out here if Samuel and all the bows and arrows are in there!"

"Okay, you've got a point," Katie conceded. Taking a deep breath, she squared her shoulders and said bravely, "Let's go, boys!"

"Besides," said Peter, noticing their strange attire. "We're all dressed for it!"

"What am I doing in a d-d-dress?" cried Matthew, shocked to see he was wearing a short leather tunic with a woven belt around his waist.

"Don't worry, boys. Look around," Katie assured them as they entered the city. "You're dressed just like everyone else your age. See those two kids over there? They look just like us."

Katie pointed down a narrow side street at a boy and girl about ten or twelve years old. Then she dropped her finger and quickly ducked her head. "Uh-oh, they're looking right at us. What are we going to do?"

"Relax, Katie," Matthew whispered under his breath. "Don't act suspicious."

"Oh, sure," muttered Katie, rolling her eyes. "I know just how kids in Zarahemla behave!"

"Hey!" Peter called happily as he waved to the other pair. "I'm Peter!"

"Oh, boy! Here we go," groaned Matthew, as Peter started toward the two strangers.

"Hi! What are your names?" he asked them, as if he talked to children from Book of Mormon days all the time.

The young boy responded with a friendly smile. "My name is Lucas, and this is my sister, Nashona."

"That's my sister, Katie, and my brother, Matthew." Peter pointed and motioned for his brother and sister to come over. "Hey, guys, come and meet Lucas and Nashona."

"Hello." Katie smiled.

"Hi," said Matthew shyly.

"Do you live here in Zarahemla?" asked Nashona.

"Uh, no. We're . . . uh . . . just visiting," stammered Matthew. "We . . . we don't really, I mean . . . um . . ."

Katie came to his rescue. "We understand that there is a prophet here named Samuel, and we wanted to hear him."

"Does that mean you are believers?" asked Lucas cautiously.

"What do you mean, believers?" wondered Katie.

"Do you believe the things the prophets teach?" Nashona responded.

"Oh, yes," said Katie with feeling. "Do you?"

"Yes, we believe with all our hearts. But most

people in Zarahemla do not believe anymore," explained Lucas sadly.

No sooner had Lucas said these words than the children heard a loud, angry commotion. A large group of shouting men were moving toward them, right down the narrow street where the children were standing. They tried to get out of the way, but there was no place to go in the tiny lane.

As the first group of men reached the children, and more people joined the mob, the children found themselves pushed roughly along the street. Peter fell to the ground, and Matthew and Katie fought to stay upright.

Afraid they would be trampled underfoot, Matthew looked around wildly, searching for a safe place. A few feet ahead, he caught sight of Lucas and Nashona huddled in a small doorway. They waved to him frantically, and he ducked into their tiny refuge. Using all his strength, he grabbed Katie as she was carried past by the mob. Then all the children shouted together for Peter, who somehow managed to squirm his way through the mass of people to the little doorway.

Relieved that they were safe for the moment, the five frightened children huddled together in a tight group. But before they could speak to one another, a few huge men—their faces darkened with paint—emerged from the crowd, dragging a man with them. The rest of the mob halted as these men ferociously shoved the man to the ground.

From their vantage point in the doorway, the

children could see the drama unfolding in the street before them.

"Get out of here," hollered one man.

"Go back to where you came from," snarled another. "We don't like your kind here!"

And then the crowd began chanting in loud, violent rhythm: "Go home, troublemaker, go home! Go home, troublemaker, go home!"

The man slowly picked himself up off the ground. Calmly, he drew his shoulders straight and lifted his face toward the fierce mob. His deep, piercing eyes seemed to look right through those who had been mocking him. Although he said nothing, he appeared so powerful, peaceful, and strong that, under his steady gaze, even the biggest men backed away and hung their heads.

And slowly, as silence fell upon the once-frenzied mob, Samuel the Lamanite, a prophet of God, walked out of the gates of Zarahemla.

Chapter Four

The Robbers' Raid

"Man!" said Peter as the crowd began leaving the street. "That was exciting!"

"You thought that was *exciting*?" Matthew asked, shaking his head. "I thought those guys were going to hurt us for sure."

"They're a mean bunch, all right," Lucas explained to Matthew. "But if you stay out of their way, they usually don't bother children much."

Then Lucas looked over at Katie and teased, "Well, we sure got a good look at Samuel, didn't we?"

"We saw him all right," said Katie, "but I never expected to risk my life while doing it!"

"Hey," said Lucas gently, noticing that Katie was still white-faced, "why don't you three come along with Nashona and me? We are going to check on our animals."

"Where are they?" Peter asked.

"They are in the fields around our home, outside the city wall," answered Nashona.

"Why do you live out there?" Peter wanted to know.

Lucas explained, "There's not enough room inside the city for pastures and crops. Most people who raise animals or food live outside. We sell vegetables in Zarahemla's chief marketplace, but we grow them out near our home."

"What's the wall really for, then?" Matthew wondered.

"It protects us from enemies," Nashona answered. "In times of trouble, we stay with our uncle inside the city."

"Who are your enemies?" Katie asked.

"You have so many questions," Lucas laughed. "Walk with us and we can talk on the way."

Katie, Matthew, and Peter followed their new friends out of the city gate into the surrounding fields.

"You were saying you have enemies . . . ," said Matthew.

"Oh, yes. There is a secret society led by an evil man named Gadianton. The society tries to make trouble for believers. We call them the Gadianton robbers," replied Lucas.

Nashona interjected excitedly, "Many of them have left the city and live in the wilderness. But some stayed right here and secretly became part of the government. They are wicked men who make unfair laws."

"What about those terrible men who were so mean to Samuel? Were they Gadianton robbers?" asked Katie.

"Some of them probably were," said Lucas, "especially the ones with painted faces. The rest were other Nephite people who have turned against the truth."

"One thing I can't understand," said Matthew, "is why a Lamanite is coming to preach to the Nephites. Isn't that backward?"

"Yes," said Nashona sadly. "A lot of Lamanites have repented and love God, while many of the Nephites have forgotten Him."

"But you haven't," said Katie.

"That's right, we haven't," said Nashona thankfully. "We believe the prophets who have taught us about Jesus Christ, the Son of God."

"But He hasn't even been born yet, right?" Matthew questioned.

"No, He hasn't, Matthew," agreed Lucas, "but we know He will be born soon. Many prophets have said so."

Nashona and Lucas approached about a dozen goats and lambs within a large fenced field. Not far away was a small dwelling made of brickwork or stone. Other animals, crops, and homes were spread over the countryside, and a few people were tending them here and there.

"These animals belong to our family," said Lucas proudly. "We keep them in this pasture to feed on the fresh grass. But we check regularly to see that they have enough to drink."

With that, Lucas removed the cork from the spout of a large rain pot. Water flowed into a long, low drinking trough. Scrambling for a place at the trough, the animals began drinking thirstily.

As the children sat petting the littlest goats, Lucas told his new friends, "When Nashona and I tend the animals, we like to sing to them. It keeps them calm. Here's one of our favorites," and he began to sing:

Our father Lehi dreamed a dream and
   God told him to go
Away from Palestine, his home, away
   from friend and foe.
And so he led his family across the desert
   sand,
Praying all the time that they would reach
   the promised land.

But faithful Nephi broke his bow and
   feared they all would starve.
Then God taught him to make new tools,
   so with them he could carve.
He made a bow and killed some beasts to
   feed the hungry band,
Still waiting for the day that they would
   reach the promised land.

Then God showed Nephi how to build a
   vessel that would float,
And carry all his family across the sea by
   boat.
Through storm and strife they sailed, protected by the mighty hand
Of Jesus Christ, their Master, 'til they
   reached the promised land.

Then Nashona joined her brother for a final verse:

Now we try our best to be as faithful as
*   they were.*
We talk of Christ, we sing of Christ. In
*   Him our hope is sure.*
And someday He will visit us, before us
*   He will stand*
In glory, as we bow to Him, here in the
*   promised land.*

Suddenly, the animals became uneasy and restless. Lucas stood and gazed at the horizon, his hand shielding his eyes.

After their harrowing morning, Katie was quick to panic. "What is it? Is there something wrong?"

"Animals sense danger long before humans do," Lucas explained with concern in his voice. "We've got to get back to the city. It might be the Gadianton robbers coming to steal from the large herds of sheep." Lucas grabbed his sister's hand. "Run as fast you can, everyone. Hurry, hurry! Follow me!"

No sooner had the five children started running, than a band of savage robbers on horseback appeared at the crest of the distant hills. As they flew across the fields, the children could hear the whoops and cries of the approaching robbers.

But Lucas was not running toward the city gate! He was running right toward the tall, solid stone wall! What was Lucas planning to do?

Just outside the wall, the children came to a grove of thick, spiky shrubs. Lucas stopped abruptly.

"What are you doing?" wailed Matthew. "We've got to keep going or they're going to get us for sure!"

"Trust me," Lucas said as he knelt on the ground and began digging. "Come on, help me dig."

"They're coming closer," warned Peter.

"Just keep digging," Lucas ordered.

In a moment, Matthew felt something solid just a few inches below the dirt, and soon a rough wooden plank appeared.

"Help me move the board," instructed Lucas.

Together, the children heaved . . . and the board came loose! Lifting it aside, they discovered what looked like a small underground cave. While four children dropped one by one into the tiny space, Lucas stayed above, covering the plank again with leaves and dirt. As he finally descended, he grabbed a rope handle on the underside of the plank and pulled it firmly back over the opening.

With the roof back in place, the cave was very dark, and the smell of damp dirt filled the children's nostrils.

"I can't see a thing," complained Katie. "How long are we going to stay here?"

"We're not going to stay here. We're going to go through a tunnel back into the city," Lucas informed her. "Get down and crawl. Follow my voice."

"Tunnel? Crawl?" whined Katie, who had never liked small spaces. "How far is it?"

"Not far," promised Lucas. "Just under the wall and into the city a bit."

"I'll have to pray the whole way!" Katie declared.

"I've had to do that before too," said Nashona, and she put a hand on Katie's back to reassure her.

"I can't wait!" cried Peter, sensing an adventure. "Let's go!"

"I guess we've got no choice," sighed Matthew. Then, sounding braver than he felt, he said, "Okay, Peter, just follow Lucas's voice."

Chapter Five

Caleb's Conversion

After a few minutes of squirming through the low, tight tunnel, the children could see faint shafts of light ahead. Moments later, Lucas pushed open a door above them, and the children emerged just inside the city wall. Covered with dirt, they brushed off each other's clothing.

Above them they could hear watchmen on top of the wall calling loudly to the city's inhabitants that the marauders were riding away. The attack was over.

"Lucas! Nashona!" The children heard the voice of a man who was hurrying toward them. "You are safe! When I heard the alarm I ran straight here from the market, praying all the way that you had made it to the tunnel. Thank heaven all is well!"

Nashona ran into the man's outstretched arms. "Father, we are so glad to see you! We were very frightened, but Lucas knew what to do."

The children's father placed his hands on Lucas's shoulders and said, "Lucas, my boy. Thank you for your quick thinking. You have kept yourself and your sister from harm today."

"And our friends, Father," Nashona cried. "This is Katie, Matthew, and Peter. They are visiting the city today, and they went with us to water the animals."

"I am happy to meet you, children," said the man warmly. "And I'm sorry you had such a scare. My name is Caleb."

"Hello," said Matthew, Katie, and Peter in unison.

"Are you here for long?" inquired Caleb.

"No," responded Katie, her mind working fast. "We're just here for the day."

"Perhaps you'd like to come with us to the market where we sell our vegetables," Caleb invited. "I need to get back to my stall."

"We would like that very much," answered Katie.

Caleb led the way through the city streets, which were beginning to quiet down after the excitement of the raid.

"Katie and her brothers are all believers, just like us," Lucas said to his father.

"That is wonderful," Caleb said in a heartfelt way. Then with some regret, he added, "I was not a believer when I was your age. That came much later in my life."

"How did you become a believer when so many other Nephites have forgotten God?" Katie asked earnestly.

"Ah," said Caleb, "that is a very good question. Let's walk this way and I will tell you of my conversion." They turned and started down a wide roadway.

"This road leads to the chief marketplace in Zarahemla," Caleb began. "One day I was walking along this very road when I heard a man praying out loud. He was obviously very worried and upset about something."

"Was he praying right here on the road?" asked Katie.

"No, he was on top of that tall tower, inside the

walls of his garden. That is his house," Caleb explained, pointing. "He was once our chief judge, you see."

"His name was Nephi, wasn't it?" Katie said, proud of herself for remembering.

"Yes, his name is Nephi." Caleb smiled. "He is named after the first Nephi, the one who left Jerusalem and sailed here to the promised land.

"As I was standing here listening to this Nephi pour out his soul to God, others heard him also, and soon many people filled this road. We all wondered why this great man seemed so troubled as he prayed.

"When Nephi finished his prayer he stood and noticed all the people gathered here. Some of those by me were rulers and judges in the land. Nephi boldly told us all to repent and believe in Christ or terrible things would happen."

"I bet the rulers didn't like hearing that!" Matthew exclaimed, shaking his head.

"They sure didn't," chuckled Caleb. "I didn't like it at first, either. But then Nephi bore his testimony. With great authority and might he proclaimed, 'Behold, I know that these things are true because the Lord God has made them known unto me.' Those words went straight to my heart, and I knew deep inside that Nephi was telling the truth."

"Did everyone there feel as you did?" asked Katie.

"Oh, no. Not at all," Caleb said, shaking his head. "In fact, many became angry—so angry that some of them said that Nephi should be put to death."

"Why would they want to kill him?" Peter asked in disbelief.

"When people choose to do wrong, they never like those who tell them what is right," said Caleb. "Have you noticed that?"

"I have," nodded Matthew. "Sometimes I get mad at my mom when she tells me I haven't done my chores. But why am I mad at her? I'm the one who did wrong. I didn't do my work!"

"Exactly!" said Caleb, who put his arm tenderly around Matthew. Then together, he and the five children walked away from the tower where a prophet of God had once prayed and began walking toward the great city of Zarahemla.

Chapter Six

A Murder Solved

As the children made their way through the stone buildings and high garden walls of Zarahemla, Caleb continued his story.

"Nephi made a prophecy to all of us gathered at his tower. He said that our chief judge, Seezoram, had just been murdered, and that he was lying in his own blood at the judgment seat," Caleb said. "We didn't believe him. How could he know that someone had just been murdered halfway across the city?"

"Was it true? Was the chief judge really dead?" asked Peter impatiently.

"Well, five men left the crowd and ran to the judgment seat. When they got there, they found Seezoram dead, just as Nephi predicted. They were so stunned by Nephi's prophetic powers, they fell to the ground in shock!

"When Seezoram's servants came in, they found the murdered chief judge and the five men lying nearby. What do you think the servants thought?"

"They thought the five men had just killed Seezoram!" cried Peter, all wound up by the suspense.

"Exactly, Peter! And the servants had the five men thrown in prison!"

"But they didn't do it!" protested Peter. "They didn't do it!"

"Right again, my boy," said Caleb. "The next day, the judges who had been at the tower heard that the five men were in prison. They knew a mistake had been made, and they ordered the men be brought to them."

"Did the five men tell the judges that Seezoram was already dead when they got there?" Katie asked.

"Yes, and the judges believed them," said Caleb.

"Whew," said Katie. "I'm glad they finally figured things out."

"Not really," said Caleb, "and things got

40

stranger still. The judges decided that Nephi must have made a plan with someone to have Seezoram killed. That way, Nephi could predict Seezoram's death and make himself look like a prophet."

"That wasn't true!" interrupted Matthew.

"No, it wasn't," agreed Caleb. "But many of the leaders and judges believed it."

"Poor Nephi!" moaned Katie. "He didn't kill anyone. He was just being a prophet!"

"True," said Caleb, "but many leaders in Zarahemla have made secret promises to destroy righteous people. They were quick to think that Nephi was guilty of murder and not a prophet after all."

"Even though you have evil leaders, you still believe in God and Jesus Christ, right?" Matthew asked Caleb.

"Yes, I do," Caleb replied with conviction.

"But why?" Katie asked. "Isn't it hard to be a believer in Zarahemla?"

Caleb thought for a moment before he responded. "You have a testimony of Jesus Christ, don't you?"

"I do," said Katie.

"Well, then you know that once you have felt the Holy Ghost swell in your heart, you can't deny it. I felt it there at Nephi's tower, so I will always believe, even though many people persecute me for it."

"Father, continue with your story or we will never get to the market," Nashona teased her father. "We are getting very hungry, you know!"

"Right you are!" Caleb laughed with understanding. "You two run ahead to Ashram's stand and get us some fruit, and we'll meet you at the vegetable stall."

"Great plan, Father!" said Lucas with a hungry gleam in his eye, and he and his sister turned onto a side street to buy fruit.

Just then, the street that Caleb and the children were traveling on widened and became an open crossroads. Pointing, Caleb continued, "It was here in this square that the multitudes gathered to hear Nephi defend himself against the wicked judges. What happened next convinced many people that Nephi was a true prophet. He gave another astonishing sign!"

"What was it?" Peter couldn't wait to hear.

"Nephi told the judges to go to the house of Seezoram's brother, Seantum, and ask him if he murdered Seezoram. Then Nephi boldly prophesied that Seantum would say unto them, Nay. And 'he shall declare unto you that he is innocent. But behold, ye shall examine him, and ye shall find blood upon the skirts of his cloak. And when ye have seen this, ye shall say: From whence cometh this blood? Do we not know that it is the blood of your brother?'"

Katie's face had become very pale at the talk of blood. Caleb lightly touched her arm.

"Katie," he said, "you look as pale as Seantum must have looked when the blood on his cloak was discovered. Nephi told the judges to say to him, 'Because of this fear and this paleness which has come upon your face, behold, we know that thou art guilty.' Nephi then prophesied that Seantum would confess that he killed his brother."

"And did it happen exactly that way?" asked astounded Matthew.

"Yes, it did," answered Caleb. "Exactly as Nephi said it would! Nephi told the judges that after all this had happened that they would then know that he was an honest man and that he was sent unto them from God.'"

"I'll bet that after that, all the people did know that he was a true prophet," said Katie.

"Some did. You remember the five men who ran to see if the chief judge had been murdered? They became converted, and they helped many believe by sharing their testimonies. Others, like me, also believed."

Caleb took a deep breath. "Well! That's the amazing story that changed my life. I felt like Lehi did in his dream when he tasted the fruit from the tree of life and wanted his family to taste it too. I couldn't wait to return home and help my family believe. Ah! Speaking of my family, look where we are."

"Father!" It was Nashona, standing behind a bright array of vegetables, while Lucas helped a woman choose some ripe ears of corn. Caleb's face lit up when he saw them.

"I guess you got the long version of the story," Lucas joked as they all came together at the vegetable stall. Then he got serious. "It is pretty miraculous, isn't it?"

"It sure is," said Matthew, his heart full of his own testimony of prophets. And when he looked over at the faces of Peter and Katie, he knew that they felt it too.

Chapter Seven

The Return of Samuel

"Come! Let us show you around the market-place!" Nashona said, after the children had enjoyed some delicious fruit and refreshing water.

The Zarahemla market was an astonishing place. Katie, Matthew, and Peter remembered visiting the market in Bethlehem. That experience had been dirty and noisy, but there were so many more people here!

Many wore beautiful clothing made from colorful, shimmering fabrics. Intricate embroidery adorned the elaborate dresses of the women. Nashona stopped at a place where heavy, ornate jewelry of glistening gold was displayed.

"Remember, we don't have money for unnecessary finery," Lucas gently reminded her.

"I know," Nashona sighed, "but I can still look."

"Come, I want to show Peter and Matthew the fantastic knives that my friend Jonas sells," Lucas said.

"Okay!" agreed Nashona enthusiastically. "Then I can show Katie the carved wooden games at the stand next to Jonas's place."

"Fair enough," Lucas replied.

The five children walked along together happily. Then, faintly, above the noise of the marketplace, the children heard shouting.

"It sounds like someone has lost his mind!" one woman muttered to her friend.

"You never know what kind of people you'll find at the market," the friend replied.

The shouting continued. "Look, up there!" A man pointed toward the top of the city wall. "There he is!"

Lucas looked up and grabbed Matthew's arm. "Matthew, it's him! It's the Lamanite prophet, Samuel. He has returned."

"Wow!" Peter said with obvious admiration.

"That's some courage, coming back after what they did to him this morning!"

The crowd quieted down in curiosity, and now Samuel's words could be heard.

"Behold, I, Samuel, a Lamanite, do speak the words of the Lord which he doth put into my heart." The crowd was silent now. "Heavy destruction awaiteth this people . . . and nothing can save this people save it be repentance and faith on the Lord Jesus Christ." Samuel's voice rang out with power.

"Who is this man and what is he talking about?" one man asked.

"He's saying that unless we repent, we're going to be destroyed," answered a richly dressed lady at his side.

"Destroyed?" the man scoffed. "Zarahemla? With the strongest wall in the world? Ha!"

Samuel continued, "The Lord hath said, 'If it were not for the righteous who are in this great city, behold, I would cause that fire should come down out of heaven and destroy it.'"

Though cries of protest were coming from the crowd, Samuel did not stop. "Your hearts are not drawn out unto the Lord, . . . and ye have sought for happiness in doing iniquity."

Just then, a boy approached the children. "Lucas!" he called.

Lucas's face lit up. "Jonas! We were just on our way to see you when Samuel started preaching from the wall. He's causing quite a stir."

"Do you know who this Lamanite is?" asked Jonas.

"Yes," Lucas answered. "He is a prophet sent to us by God."

"A prophet?" questioned Jonas doubtfully. "How do you know that?"

Lucas looked at his friend. "I cannot prove it to you, Jonas, but you can learn for yourself, just as I did."

"How?" asked Jonas.

"Listen to his words very carefully," Lucas encouraged him. "And then you must pray to God, asking Him if what Samuel says is true."

"God is not going to speak to me," Jonas insisted.

"Well, maybe not in words, Jonas," Lucas said, looking directly into Jonas's eyes. "But God will make your heart swell with the feeling that Samuel is His prophet."

Matthew couldn't hold back any longer. "Jonas," he said earnestly, "you do not know me, but I can tell you that what Lucas says is true. If you pray, God will teach you the truth in your heart."

After a long moment, Jonas replied. "All right," he said quietly. "I will do that." And then he turned thoughtfully toward the wall where brave Samuel was still preaching God's word to the people.

Chapter Eight

A Narrow Escape

"Behold, I give unto you a sign; for five years more cometh, and behold, then cometh the Son of God to redeem all those who shall believe on his name. . . . There shall be one day and a night and a day, as if it were one day and there were no night; and this shall be unto you for a sign; for ye shall know of the rising of the sun and also of its setting; therefore they shall know of a surety that there shall be two days and a night; nevertheless the night shall not be darkened; and it shall be the night before he is born." Samuel prophesied with a thundering, but somehow peaceful voice.

"A day and a night and a day—with no darkness at all?" Jonas questioned in disbelief. "How could that happen?"

"It will be a miracle of God," explained Lucas quietly. "A sign to us that the Savior, Jesus Christ, is going to be born far across the sea."

Samuel went on. "And behold, there shall a new star arise, such an one as ye never have beheld; and this also shall be a sign unto you."

"How I'd like to see that," said Jonas longingly.

Just then, a large group of protesters surged through the crowd, pushing people out of the way as they went. They carried large crossbows with arrows already aimed toward the wall.

"Look at those bows," whispered Peter. "Do you think they're going to use them?"

"Without thinking twice!" answered Lucas ominously.

"This is the end for you, Lamanite," the ringleader yelled savagely to Samuel. Then he began barking directions to the men in his group. "You with the bows, stay here and fire. The rest of you, throw whatever rocks you can find. Knock him off the wall!"

Samuel stood firm, still fearlessly shouting out his message as if he knew he would be protected by God.

Enraged, many clambered for rocks to throw. As the stones began to fly upward and the arrows sailed through the air, Lucas yelled, "Run! Follow me!" All the children scrambled frantically to get away from the danger.

But Peter, worried for Samuel, stopped at a pile of stones that the people had gathered to throw. Quietly, he grabbed as many as he could and then turned to run.

One of the largest men realized what Peter was doing and roared, "It's a believer!" And with one swoop of his massive arm, he had Peter in his clutches. Peter dropped the stones and squirmed with all his might, but he couldn't break free.

Matthew grabbed Katie. "Katie, listen to me! You've got to hold my hand with all your might. Don't let go no matter what! We have to get Peter out of here!"

Swallowing her fear, Katie nodded with determination. Peter was still flailing in the man's arms, but try as the man might, he could not quite contain Peter's wiry, thrashing body.

"Give me some rope to tie him up," he ordered the other men. "This is a feisty one."

Matthew's heart was pounding with fear. Holding tight to Katie's hand, he lunged forward with all his might and grabbed blindly for Peter. He got only Peter's foot.

"Peter," he yelled, "your hand! Give me your hand!"

Desperately, Matthew lunged again. Somehow, in the struggle, their hands met and Matthew grabbed hold for everything he was worth. As the hands of the three children connected, they felt their feet leave the ground. The air rushed around them, and they seemed for a moment to hover in space. Then in an instant, they were safe at Grandma's feet. And Grandma, without so much as a glance their way, was still reading!

Chapter Nine

In Five Years' Time

Savoring the safety of Grandma's peaceful cottage, the children breathed deeply in relief, listening to her soothing voice read on about the scene they had just left.

To Katie's great joy, Grandma read that the stones and arrows simply could not hit Samuel. But then, the frustrated Nephites decided to try to bind him with ropes and take him away.

"'And as they went forth to lay their hands on him, behold, he did cast himself down from the wall, and did flee out of their lands, yea, even unto his own country, and began to preach and to prophesy among his own people.'"

Katie felt a wave of happiness. Samuel was safe! She looked over at her two brothers, smiling . . .

and her heart stopped. The boys were still wearing their Zarahemla clothes! Then she looked down at herself. She, too, was wearing her embroidered cloth gown from more than two thousand years ago!

"Matthew," she whispered softly so Grandma wouldn't hear and gave him a nudge.

"Oh!" he gasped, wide-eyed with surprise at her attire.

"Shh," Katie cautioned, putting her finger to her lips.

Matthew pointed to the blankets between them on the floor. The two children covered themselves quickly, concealing their strange clothing. Then Katie gently wrapped another blanket around Peter, who smiled at his sister and pulled it around his shoulders, unaware of its real purpose.

Grandma's voice continued, "'And behold, he was never heard of more among the Nephites.' My, what a story, children!" she exclaimed.

"You can say that again!" Peter replied.

Grandma looked down at the three children all wrapped up in blankets.

"Oh dear, is it that cold in here? I was so caught

up in the story, I didn't notice," she said. "I'll get another log for the fire."

Grandma headed outside to the woodpile.

"What are we going to do?" Matthew asked in a worried voice.

"We've got to get our own clothes back somehow," answered Katie.

"Our own clothes?" Peter questioned. "Well, what are we wearing now?" As he flung off his

blanket, he was shocked at the sight of the leather tunic still tied around his body.

The children heard rustling at the door, and Katie squealed, "Quick, Peter! Cover up!"

"Here we go," Grandma said cheerily as she entered the cottage and fed the fire. "I want you to stay nice and warm so that we can finish the story."

"I thought the story was finished. Samuel left and was never heard from again," Katie reminded Grandma.

"It's true that we don't hear any more about Samuel, but what about the believers who were left behind?" Grandma asked.

For the first time since their escape from Zarahemla, the children thought about Lucas, Nashona, Caleb, and Jonas. Had they been able to get away from the angry crowd without getting caught? Where were they now? Did Jonas pray for a testimony as he said he would?

"I guess I wasn't thinking about them," admitted Matthew.

"Well, the best part of the story is yet to come," Grandma promised.

"Did the Nephites repent?" Katie asked hopefully.

"What happened to the Gadianton robbers? Did they ever go to jail?" Peter wanted to know.

"Did any of the people listening end up believing Samuel?" asked Matthew, thinking of Jonas.

"Well, I can see you've been listening to the story," smiled Grandma. "Here's what happened. Most people still didn't believe that Christ would come. After all, why would He be born in a land far away where they could not see Him with their own eyes? They thought that surely this must be a trick to get them to believe in something that was not true."

"But the prophets were telling the truth," said Matthew.

"That's the way it is with prophets. You have to listen with your heart as well as your ears to believe the message," Grandma said.

"Yeah, and if you don't, old Satan can really get hold of you," Peter observed.

"You've learned a lot for someone your age," Grandma said. "That is exactly how it was. Satan really had hold of many of the Nephites."

She picked up her scriptures again. "Let's find out what happened in Zarahemla five years later."

Grandma started to read. "'But there were some who began to say that the time was past for the words to be fulfilled, which were spoken by Samuel, the Lamanite. And they began to rejoice over their brethren, saying: Behold the time is past, and the words of Samuel are not fulfilled; therefore, your joy and your faith concerning this thing hath been vain.

"'. . . and the people who believed began to be very sorrowful, lest by any means those things which had been spoken might not come to pass.

"'But behold, they did watch steadfastly for that day and that night and that day which should be as one day as if there were no night, . . .

"'Now it came to pass that there was a day set apart by the unbelievers, that all those who believed in those traditions should be put to death except the sign should come to pass, which had been given by Samuel the prophet.'"

Put to death! Matthew's heart sank. He looked at Katie, who was thinking the same thing. What would become of Lucas and Nashona? And kind Caleb?

Suddenly Grandma's painting caught Katie's eye. The tiny people were once again moving through the city! Matthew saw it too. Even Peter sat still long enough to notice.

And suddenly, Matthew knew just what they should do. With great feeling, he whispered to his siblings, "Let's go back!"

"I'm not sure I want to," Katie said hesitantly, remembering the frightening events of their last visit.

"We've got to get our clothes back somehow," Matthew implored. "Maybe this is how. Let's try it. Please!"

"Yeah," agreed Peter. "We can always come back, Katie. We'll stick close together, I promise."

"I must be crazy, but . . . okay." Katie gave in. She ached to know if Caleb and his family were okay in spite of all the persecution they faced.

"Peter, are you ready?" Matthew softly asked.

Peter grinned. "I'm always ready for an adventure, big brother!"

"Hold on," said Matthew as they locked hands.

And he eagerly reached up to thrust his hand into the enchanted picture of the city they now knew well. In a flash, they were swallowed by the landscape and were on the way back to Zarahemla, wondering just what they would find there.

Chapter Ten

When the Night Stayed Bright as Day

The return to Zarahemla was swift and un-eventful, which was a great relief to Katie. The city was quiet in comparison to the chaos they had left when Samuel was delivering his warning. Still dressed in their Zarahemla clothes, the children walked through the crowds at the ancient market.

"Let's go to Caleb's vegetable stall and see if he's there," Katie proposed.

"It's right down this way, isn't it?" motioned Peter.

But when they arrived at the stall, an unfamiliar man stood behind a display of woven baskets. "Do you know where Caleb is?" Matthew asked, ap-proaching the man.

"Ha! Caleb is not here anymore," he sneered, his voice full of hatred. "We don't like his kind."

"His kind?" Peter was puzzled.

"Believers!" He said the word with disgust. "But we're gonna be rid of those pests."

"Rid of them? How?" asked Katie.

"Where have you been?" the man asked rudely. "For five years we have listened to the believers talk about a sign from God. Has it come? No! There's been no sign, and tomorrow the believers will be put to death—unless there's a night without any darkness! Ha, ha, ha!" He laughed with a snarl that alarmed Katie.

"Come on," she whispered to Matthew. "Let's get out of here."

Matthew began backing away from the man. "Thanks," he said with a polite smile. "We need to get going."

The children slowly rounded the nearest corner and then started running until they felt safe again.

"Let's walk over to Nephi's garden," Matthew suggested. "Maybe some of the believers are there."

"That's a good idea," Katie agreed.

"Great!" said Peter with enthusiasm. "I can't wait to see that big tower again!"

The children walked along the wide roadway that would take them past Nephi's house near the center of the sprawling city. They passed many other travelers along the way. Katie looked at each of them with great interest, wondering if any of them were believers.

She pointed to a mother with two small children walking just ahead of them. "See that sweet-looking woman?" she asked her brothers. "I'll bet she's a believer!"

"I'll go see!" Peter darted ahead to the woman before Katie and Matthew could stop him. Both held their breath, wondering what their bubbly little brother was going to say.

"Hi! My name's Peter! Are you believers?"

The woman held her children close to her side, looking around to see if anyone else had heard Peter's question.

"Why do you want to know?" she asked cautiously.

"Well, we're believers, and my sister here

thought maybe you were too," Peter explained with a friendly smile.

Katie drew closer. "I guess you've met my brother," she reassured the frightened woman.

"Yes, I have," she answered warily. "You should be more careful about announcing that you're believers. Some people would want to hurt you."

"You mean the Gadianton robbers?" asked wide-eyed Peter.

"Yes," the woman nodded, "and others."

"We looked for another believer named Caleb at the market, but his stand wasn't there anymore. Do you know him?" Katie asked.

"If he was the one who once sold vegetables there, I know who he is. He hasn't worked there for quite some time," the woman answered with some sadness. "These are perilous times for the believers."

"Do you know where we might find him?" asked Matthew, wanting to know if his friends were okay.

"Some of us are gathering to pray. Perhaps he will be there," the woman suggested. "Would you like to come along?"

The three children nodded gratefully.

They followed the woman along a familiar route. Soon, just ahead, a tower appeared. They were at Nephi's garden! Many were gathered within its walls, talking to one another in hushed tones.

One man stepped to the center of the group, raising both hands to quiet everyone. Then he spoke.

"We have watched steadfastly for that day and a night and a day which should be as one day. Five years have passed since Samuel, the Lamanite prophet, made that prophecy. Today, we are gathered to ask the Lord to send this sign so that we might not be put to death."

All of the people knelt and bowed their heads as the man offered a long, pleading prayer. At the end of the prayer, families solemnly embraced.

"Matthew," Peter grabbed him by the arm. "Isn't that Caleb over there?"

"Yes, I think it is," Matthew answered, seeing Caleb through the crowd. "Hey, that's Lucas and Nashona with him! I almost didn't recognize them. They're practically grown-ups!"

Then Matthew pointed to a tall, fine-looking

young man standing near Lucas. "And who is that with them? He looks familiar, too."

"Oh, Matthew," said Katie, her voice choking with tears. "It's Jonas!"

"Jonas!" repeated Matthew, recognizing the boy who had doubted Samuel's words. "He believes!"

"Let's go say hello," Peter suggested.

"Wait, boys," Katie cautioned. "I don't think that would be a good idea. They are all five years older—but we're not. We'd have a lot of explaining to do. Besides, it looks as if they are leaving the garden now."

"Maybe we could just walk behind and watch them for a bit," Matthew suggested.

As the sun began to set along the horizon, the children walked westward through the city, following many of the believers. The buildings of Zarahemla, reflecting the sun's golden rays, seemed to glow from within. Matthew was quiet as he watched Caleb and his family walk in front of them.

"What are you thinking?" Katie wanted to know.

"I'm wondering how Jonas must feel. Five years

ago, he didn't believe in Jesus Christ. Now, he could be killed tomorrow because of his testimony!"

It was Katie's turn to be quiet, thinking about her friend Nashona. What if Katie were in Nashona's place? Would she be faithful enough to trust a prophet, even if it cost her life?

In silent prayer, the children walked through the streets of Zarahemla, overwhelmed by the faith of their believing friends.

Slowly the sun disappeared behind the horizon.

But strangely, the glow in the city continued undimmed. Suddenly a chorus of joyful cries could be heard, louder and louder as it rippled through the city.

All around, people were pointing toward the sky. Indeed, the sun was gone, but the sky was as bright as day! It was as light as if the sun had never set!

Before long, some of those on the road began to moan in dismay, and they fell to the earth as if they were dead.

But Caleb's family and the other believers reacted very differently to the miracle of light. In indescribable joy, they fell to their knees, tears running down their faces.

"We are saved!" Nashona wept. "Our prayers have been answered."

And Jonas cried with his arms outstretched toward heaven, "Glory be to God! The Savior of the world is coming to the earth!"

"Matthew, this is it," Katie said quietly. "This is the sign that Samuel said would come."

"The sun is gone, but the world is full of light," Matthew marveled.

"And all the believers look so happy!" Peter observed, overcome by the spirit encircling the land of Zarahemla and filling his heart to overflowing.

Tenderly, Katie took Peter's hand and reached out for Matthew's. "Shall we return to Grandma?"

"Wait just a minute, Katie," Matthew said. "I never want to forget this." He took one long last look at their friends offering prayers of thanksgiving to God. Then he gazed upward to the nighttime sky, filled with light and bright as day. When he felt the picture was impressed forever on his mind and the wonder was fixed forever in his heart, he reached out for his sister's hand.

Chapter Eleven

Home Again

"'And it came to pass also that a new star did appear, according to the word. . . . And thus the ninety and second year did pass away, bringing glad tidings unto the people because of the signs which did come to pass. . . .'" Grandma finished reading.

"Well, that is quite an end to a very exciting story, wouldn't you say?" she said. "Are you children still cold?"

Katie hardly dared to look under her blanket for fear that her everyday clothes had not reappeared. She glanced over at Matthew who had a worried look on his face too. But before they could say anything, Peter threw off his blanket.

"I'm not cold anymore!" he exclaimed.

Katie's heart skipped a beat, but to her great relief, Peter was no longer in his Zarahemla clothes.

Katie peeked under her blanket and discovered that she, too, was in the same clothes she had worn to Grandma's. And Matthew was in the jeans and T-shirt he had put on after his soccer practice. Was it earlier today that he had been on the soccer field with his friends? So much had happened since then!

"Grandma, did you know they were going to kill all the people who believed that Jesus was going to be born?" Peter asked her.

Grandma laughed. "I just read the story to you, you know."

"Oh yeah, silly me," he blushed. "What would they have done if the sign hadn't appeared?"

"I guess we'll never know, will we?" said Grandma.

"It must have been hard for Samuel to go and tell the Nephites that what they were doing was wrong," Matthew observed.

"I have a friend at school that had to tell her friends she wasn't going to hang around with them because they were cheating on tests and skipping classes," Katie told Grandma.

"That took a lot of courage," replied Grandma.

"They've been kind of mean to her ever since," Katie said sadly.

"Yeah!" said Matthew. "When people do something wrong, they want you to do it too. And if you don't, they get really mad and they don't like you anymore."

"Hey, that's just like the Gadianton robbers," Peter added.

Grandma was beaming. "Did you know that the Book of Mormon says we should 'liken all scriptures unto us, that it might be for our profit and learning'?"

"I've heard that before, but what does it mean?" Matthew wanted to know.

"It means you should think about your own life as you read the scriptures. Then the stories in the scriptures can give you ideas about how to be more righteous and true," Grandma told them.

"You mean that we can be like Samuel and stand up for what we believe?" Katie asked.

"Yes, that is one thing," replied Grandma.

"How about this one?" Matthew ventured. "Sometimes you can be right, even if most other people think you're not."

"That's another good one," said Grandma.

"And you shouldn't be mean like the Gadianton robbers!" said Peter. The Gadianton robbers had obviously made a big impression on him.

"Exactly!" Grandma told him. "Why don't you take out your journals and write down all these things so that you'll always remember what you have learned."

Matthew and Katie began writing furiously. They wanted to record everything that had transpired that day: Meeting Lucas, Nashona, and Caleb. Jonas becoming a believer. Samuel prophesying on the wall. And, of course, the sign in the sky that Jesus would be born.

"Grandma, how do you spell 'prophet'?" Peter asked, snuggling next to her. As she slipped her arm around her youngest grandson, a favorite scripture filled her heart: "I have no greater joy than to hear that my children walk in truth." She looked with wonder at each of her grandchildren, grateful they were learning to love the scriptures!

Peter interrupted her reverie. "Grandma, have you ever seen a Gadianton robber?"

"Uh, um . . . ," Grandma stammered. "Well . . . in a way, I guess. I mean, I put some here in my painting, shooting at Samuel . . ."

"Oh, yeah," said Peter, "and you know, they're even meaner than they look!"

"Well, I'd have to agree with you there!" Grandma responded with certainty.

"You would? So you have seen one?" asked Peter

"Well . . . Oh, my! Look at the fire! It's almost out. I'll go get another log while you keep writing in your journals." And she headed out the door.

Meanwhile, her three grandchildren looked at each other, utterly bewildered. After a moment, they shook their heads, shrugged their shoulders, and then continued writing. But Peter's question, still unanswered, lingered in the air about them as they wrote, and they wondered: Was Grandma keeping a secret too?

About the Authors

Alice W. Johnson, a published author and composer, is a featured speaker for youth groups, adult firesides, and women's seminars. A former executive in a worldwide strategy consulting company, and then in a leadership training firm, Alice is now a homemaker living in Eagle, Idaho, with her husband and their four young children.

Allison H. Warner gained her early experience living with her family in countries around the world. Returning to the United States as a young woman, she began her vocation as an actress and writer, developing and performing in such productions as *The Farley Family Reunion*. She and her husband reside in Provo, Utah, where they are raising two active boys.

About the Illustrators

Jerry Harston held a degree in graphic design and illustrated more than thirty children's books. He received many honors for his art, and his clients included numerous Fortune 500 corporations. Jerry passed away in December 2009.

Casey Nelson grew up the oldest of eight children in a Navy family, so they moved quite often during her childhood. Graduating with a degree in illustration, she taught figure drawing in the illustration department at Brigham Young University, worked as an artist for video games, and performed in an improvisational comedy troupe. Casey is employed by the Walt Disney Company as a cinematic artist for their video games.